A CourseGuide for

Know How We Got Our Bible

Ryan M. Reeves
Charles E. Hill

ZONDERVAN
ACADEMIC

ZONDERVAN ACADEMIC

A CourseGuide for Know How We Got Our Bible
Copyright © 2020 by Zondervan

Requests for information should be addressed to:
Zondervan, *3900 Sparks Dr. SE, Grand Rapids, Michigan 49546*

ISBN 978-0-310-11092-7 (softcover)

Printed in the United States of America

CONTENTS

Introduction

Welcome to *A CourseGuide for Know How We Got Our Bible*. These guides were created for formal and informal students alike who want to engage deeper in biblical, theological, or ministry studies. We hope this guide will provide an opportunity for you to grow not only in your understanding, but also in your faith.

How to Use This Guide

This guide is meant to be used in conjunction with the book *Know How We Got Our Bible* and its corresponding videos, *Know How We Got Our Bible Video Study*. After you have read each chapter in the book and watched the accompanying video lesson, the materials in this guide will help you review and assess what you have learned. Application-oriented questions are included as well.

Each CourseGuide has been individually designed to best equip you in your studies, but in general, you can expect the following components. Most CourseGuides begin every chapter with a "You Should Know" section, which highlights key terminology, people, and facts to remember. This section serves as a helpful summary for directing your studies. Reflection questions, typically two to three per chapter, prompt you to summarize key points you've learned. Discussion questions invite you to an even deeper level of engagement. Finally, most chapters will end with a short quiz to test your retention. You can find the answer key to each quiz at the bottom of the page following it.

For Further Study

CourseGuides accompany books and videos from some of the world's top biblical and theological scholars. They may be used independently,

or in small groups or classrooms, offering quality instruction to
equip students for academic and ministry pursuits. If you would like
to engage in further study with Zondervan's CourseGuides, the full
lineup may be viewed online. After completing your studies with *A
CourseGuide for Know How We Got Our Bible*, we recommend moving
on to *A CourseGuide for Know the Creeds and Councils* and *A Course-
Guide for Know the Heretics*.

CHAPTER 1

Who's on First

You Should Know

- Most Christians over the centuries never had personal Bibles.

- Perhaps the most important change in our lifetime is our access to the Bible.

- One question that Christians often ask about the Bible is if all Bible translations are the same.

- Christians often ask if the text of the Bible is trustworthy.

- The aim of the dynamic-equivalent translation method is to provide parallel ideas.

- Scholars who study biblical manuscripts in order to reconstruct the autographs as closely as possible are known as textual critics.

Essay Questions

Short

1. Describe the ways in which ancient Bibles were unlike our modern Bibles.

2. What was the criteria the Israelites used for recognizing that a book was to be included in the Old Testament canon?

3. What conclusions can we draw from the research of textual critics concerning the reliability of the Bible?

Long

1. Explain how comparing multiple English Bible translations can help you to better understand the meaning of a Bible passage than if you used only one translation.

Quiz

1. (T/F) Even seminary students occasionally admit they wish they knew more of the basics.

2. (T/F) The Bibles we own are very much like those in the early church.

3. In what ways are the Bibles we own different from ancient Bibles?
   a) The shape of it
   b) The size of it
   c) The arrangement of the books
   d) All of the above

4. (T/F) Most medieval Christians owned a Latin Vulgate Bible.

5. (T/F) Translating the Bible as closely as possible to the original text is called the phrase-for-phrase method.

6. (T/F) The dynamic-equivalent method of translation seeks to avoid wooden or confusing wording, even if it means ignoring the precise wording of the original document.

7. The most common translation method used for works of literature is which of the following methods?
   a) Word-for-word translation
   b) Literal translation
   c) Dynamic-equivalence translation
   d) Paraphrase

8. (T/F) A word-for-word translation never uses the dynamic-equivalent method.

9. (T/F) In the Reformation era, European scholars had a smaller number of biblical manuscripts than have been found today.

10. (T/F) The text of the Bible is not as well attested as most ancient books.

CHAPTER 2

The Old Testament

You Should Know

- The most significant difference between the Jewish Bible and the modern Old Testament is their arrangement.
- The Torah was the foundation of the covenant God made with Israel.
- The Sadducees followed only the Torah.
- The book of Daniel does not belong to the Prophets section of the Jewish canon.
- Tanakh: the Jewish canon in its entirety, the same as our Old Testament
- The Council of Jamnia affirmed the Jewish canon.

Essay Questions

Short

1. Why was the Torah considered to be the basis for the rest of the Old Testament? Why is the Pentateuch always the first five books of the Bible? (p. 33–34)

2. Describe briefly the arrangement of the books in the section of the Jewish canon called the Prophets.

3. Describe briefly the arrangement of the books in the section of the Jewish canon called the Writings.

Long

1. In what way does the finding of the Dead Sea Scrolls help to establish the accuracy of the later Hebrew manuscripts?

Quiz

1. (T/F) The Old Testament refers to the old covenant God made with Israel.

2. (T/F) Christians frequently learned the Hebrew language prior to the Renaissance.

3. From what time period are the manuscript copies upon which the text of our Old Testament is based?
   - a) Prior to the destruction of Jerusalem in AD 70
   - b) From during the Middle Ages
   - c) From after the Renaissance
   - d) From the time of Moses

4. (T/F) All significant editions of the Hebrew Bible today are based primarily on the Leningrad Codex.

5. (T/F) The Aleppo and Leningrad Codex are both written on scrolls rather than in book format.

6. (T/F) The discovery of the Dead Sea Scrolls provides relatively few new insights into the Old Testament.

7. Which Old Testament book was not found at Qumran?
   - a) Job
   - b) Esther
   - c) Psalms
   - d) Isaiah

8. (T/F) The *Torah* refers specifically to the Ten Commandments.

9. Into how many books is the Old Testament Prophets section combined in the Jewish canon?
   - a) Twenty-one
   - b) Twelve
   - c) Eight
   - d) Twenty-seven

10. (T/F) The Tanakh refers to the first section of the Jewish canon.

CHAPTER 3

The Septuagint and Apocrypha

You Should Know

- The cultural influence of the Greeks spilled down into the streets, creating *koine* Greek, a form of Greek that was used in the marketplace.

- The legend of the seventy-two Jewish scribes who translated the Hebrew Old Testament in Greek is found in the Letter of Aristeas.

- The Septuagint was translated over centuries, by a variety of translators.

- When it comes to the Septuagint: the first portion was translated at least by the middle of the second century BC; the Septuagint is the oldest translation of the Hebrew text; the Septuagint employs a different book arrangement than is used in the Hebrew Bible; and texts from outside the Jewish canon were included in the Septuagint

- The influence of the Septuagint was felt especially in the Eastern church, later known as the Orthodox Church, which to this day maintains the Septuagint as its Scriptures.

- When it comes to the influence of the Septuagint during the time of the early church: early Christians needed a Greek translation because they did not know Hebrew; some Christians cited books from the Apocrypha during their debates with Jews; some Jews resisted the popularity of the Septuagint; Origen argued in favor of using the Septuagint

Essay Questions

Short

1. Describe the historical events that, according to legend, led to the translation of the Septuagint. Explain why the Septuagint is a significant translation.

2. What are some reasons why books outside of the canon of Scripture were included in the Septuagint?

3. Discuss how the Septuagint influenced early Christianity.

Long

1. What are some ways in which the Septuagint has affected our modern Bibles?

Quiz

1. (T/F) The spread of Jewish culture during the Jewish Diaspora led to the first translation of the Old Testament.

2. (T/F) The Jews living outside of Jerusalem became increasingly dependent on the Greek language for everyday life.

3. (T/F) The most enduring legacy of Alexander's conquests was the Greek language.

4. (T/F) The Letter of Aristeas is a historically-accurate account of the translation of the Septuagint, written by the real Aristeas.

5. (T/F) The Septuagint was translated over centuries, by a variety of translators.

6. (T/F) Perhaps the most important influence of the Septuagint on our Bibles is the arrangement of its books.

7. (T/F) The Septuagint only includes texts that are considered to be in the Jewish canon.

8. (T/F) The Orthodox Church uses the Septuagint as its Scriptures.

9. (T/F) Many Jews resisted the popularity of the Septuagint.

10. (T/F) Origen argued in favor of going back to the Jewish canon.

CHAPTER 4

The New Testament

You Should Know

- The events of the sending of the Holy Spirit and the incarnation of Jesus are at the heart of the New Testament.

- The books of the New Testament are arranged according to genre and then often according to size.

- Characteristics of the Synoptic Gospels: tell the story of the life, death, and resurrection of Christ; are the earliest Gospels written; work together; probably use one another in their composition

- The writing of the Gospel of John contains short sentences and basic syntax.

- Paul's writings cover various topics.

- Apostolic authority was one of the most important issues for the early church.

Essay Questions

Short

1. Why did the Jews find it blasphemous for Jesus to accept the worship and obedience of his followers?

2. Why was it important that Jesus sent out his apostles beginning from Jerusalem?

3. What information do we gain from early church traditions about the New Testament books?

Long

1. In what way would the apostolic authority transfer to a letter sent from an apostle? How would the churches respond to receiving a letter from an apostle?

Quiz

1. (T/F) Jesus accepting the worship and obedience of his followers was a common expectation for a Jewish rabbi.

2. (T/F) The glory of the Lord departing from the temple was a sign of God's withdrawing his presence from Israel and of their coming judgment in exile.

3. (T/F) The "Second Temple period" means the time during the New Testament time period.

4. (T/F) The Jewish leaders' oral law began to be developed after the birth of Christ.

5. (T/F) God no longer sent prophets during the time between the Old and New Testaments.

6. (T/F) It is possible to date with precision each of the New Testament books.

7. (T/F) The Gospels come first because Christ's ministry is the foundation of the new covenant.

8. Which Gospel do many scholars believe was written first?
   a) Matthew
   b) Mark
   c) Luke
   d) John

9. (T/F) The Catholic Epistles are called this because they are used predominantly by the Roman Catholic Church.

10. (T/F) Apostolic authority was one of the most important issues in the early church for recognizing that a book was canonical.

CHAPTER 5

The Earliest Christians

You Should Know

- New Testament books that were disputed in the early church: James, Jude, 2 Peter, 2 and 3 John

- The four categories for the discussion of the New Testament canon: Received books, Rejected books, Disputed books, and Heretical books

- The church assumed a canon long before they developed the grammar and language to describe the canon.

- The earliest evidence in Christian writings suggests that the adoption of the Apocrypha was not universal.

- Justin wrote several works that defended Christians.

- The fact that certain books would be disputed shows that the early church knew that only inspired books belong to the New Testament.

Essay Questions

Short

1. What was the main concern about the disputed New Testament books? What is a possible reason why certain books of the New Testament were disputed?

2. Why were New Testament books accepted into the canon? Is this reason enough to counter the concerns of a few who disputed the book?

3. What do the testimonies of Justin, Theophilus, and Melito say about the reception of the Apocrypha in the early church? Was it an intentional choice for many Christians to eventually accept the Apocrypha as canonical? If not, how did it happen?

Long

1. How does the concept of canonicity give you confidence to trust that you have in your possession all the revelation that God wants to give to you?

Quiz

1. (T/F) Because of the coming of the New Testament, some Jewish believers questioned the canonicity of some Old Testament books.

2. Which of the following New Testament books were thought by some in the early church to not have been written by the authors ascribed to them?

    a) James
    b) Jude
    c) 3 John
    d) All of the above

3. (T/F) For a New Testament book to be disputed is another way of saying that the book was rejected by the majority of churches.

4. (T/F) The Gospel of Thomas is a disputed book.

5. (T/F) For discussion of the New Testament canon, it is most important to recognize that nearly all of the books were always on the "accepted" list.

6. (T/F) The earliest evidence in Christian writings suggests that the adoption of the Apocrypha into the canon was universal.

7. (T/F) Jerome was shocked to learn that the Jews did not accept the Apocrypha as canonical.

8. (T/F) Today, Eastern Orthodox churches are beginning to dispute the Apocrypha as being inspired and should not remain as part of their Bibles.

9. (T/F) Many people assume that there was no fixed New Testament canon until centuries after the first century.

10. (T/F) The church's assumption is that the canon is something received, not something they created.

CHAPTER 6

The Vulgate

You Should Know

- The Latin Vulgate was translated in the fourth century by Jerome.
- The Vulgate was seen as a newfangled translation that was disrespectful to the Septuagint.
- Jerome was secretary to Pope Damasus I; studied Greek, Hebrew, and Latin; at times lived as a hermit in the desert; and enjoyed living a life of pleasure
- Arianism taught: the Son is exalted above angels; the Son is exalted above human beings; the Son is a created being; and the Son is not of the same essence as the Father
- Items necessary for a successful translation: a translator who is skilled and has a scholarly mind; financial support for the project; church support so that the translation will be used in the churches
- By the early fourth century, nearly all major works of theology were written in Greek.

Essay Questions

Short

1. What major life events led Jerome to Christian asceticism? While living as a hermit, what tool did Jerome gain that would be used in his study of the Bible?

2. There were great theological controversies in the church of Jerome's day. Instead of writing to defend orthodoxy, what task did Jerome consider to be more important?

3. What was Jerome's view of the Apocrypha?

Long

1. Describe the Old Latin translations and why a new Latin translation was needed. What are some reasons why churches held on to their Old Latin Bibles and did not accept Jerome's Vulgate?

Quiz

1. (T/F) At one time the Catholic Church condemned the use of any translation except the Latin Vulgate.

2. (T/F) The Vulgate obtained almost immediate reception by the Western church.

3. (T/F) Jerome was an intellectual man who rejected the Christian faith.

4. (T/F) Jerome studied Greek and Latin, but never Hebrew.

5. (T/F) Early Latin translations were often poor attempts to translate the Bible.

6. (T/F) All Old Latin translations are identical or nearly identical.

7. (T/F) Jerome translated the books of the Apocrypha using the Septuagint.

8. (T/F) The translation method used for the Vulgate is dynamic-equivalency.

9. (T/F) There are few surviving copies of the Vulgate from centuries immediately after Jerome.

10. (T/F) The church ceased using the Old Latin translations as soon as the Vulgate became available.

CHAPTER 7

The Medieval Bible

You Should Know

- One of the main goals of the Carolingian Renaissance was to formalize the use of Latin among scholars and churchmen.

- The features included at the palace of Aachen: a library, a Roman bath, a scriptorium, and monkeys

- Some of the items that were produced at Aachen that were sent throughout Europe: regulations for church and state, official documents, famous scholarly works, copies of the Bible

- Alcuin promoted the Latin Vulgate because Latin was the language of choice; Latin was used by intellectuals; Latin was the language used in classical Rome

- The Carolingian Renaissance created a new style of handwriting.

- The Bible during the medieval period was copied in several different formats.

Essay Questions

Short

1. How did the lack of official sanction for the Vulgate affect its reception? How did later scribes circumvent the problem that the Vulgate did not contain the Apocrypha?

2. What kingdoms did Charlemagne seek to revive, at least concerning their glory and intellectual pursuits?

3. Explain why it was so expensive to produce Bibles during the medieval period.

Long

1. For what reason would Latin have been chosen as the primary language for academic work at Aachen? What effect would this have on scholarship in many countries? How did this choice promote the use of the Vulgate?

Quiz

1. (T/F) The Carolingian Renaissance sought to formalize the use of Latin among scholars and churchmen.

2. (T/F) The Carolingian scholars sought to perpetuate the use of the Old Latin translations.

3. (T/F) Later scribes began to introduce translations of the Apocrypha into the Vulgate.

4. (T/F) Charlemagne established a library that was equipped to produce copies of the Bible.

5. (T/F) Latin was experiencing a resurgence in Europe by the time Alcuin started working for Charlemagne.

6. Which of the following was the purpose for developing the Carolingian miniscule script?
    a) To make the text easier to read
    b) To champion the use of the Latin Vulgate
    c) To lower the chance of errors by copyists
    d) To make it easier for children to write

7. (T/F) Most medieval Bibles were produced in a single volume.

8. (T/F) One of the most useful medieval Bibles is *Codex Gigas*, or the Giant Bible.

9. (T/F) Medieval Bibles were relatively cheap because cow and sheep skins were easy to obtain.

10. (T/F) The most important innovation for producing Bibles was the invention of movable-type printing.

CHAPTER 8

The Renegade Bible of John Wycliffe

You Should Know

- The Lollard movement rode alongside social change in England where the peasants and middle class called for social change.

- The expansion of papal authority was first designed to thwart a series of kings who would not listen to the church.

- Pope Gregory VII issued a series of blistering decrees, called *Dictatus Papae*, that threatened to dethrone any political ruler who interfered with Catholic business.

- Wycliffe was comfortable with Latin, Anglo-Norman, and Middle English.

- Wycliffe lived in North Riding Yorkshire in northern England, studied at Oxford, and was influenced by Bradwardine's book *On the Cause of God against the Pelagians*.

- Early in Wycliffe's life he was preoccupied with the return of Christ.

Essay Questions

Short

1. Why was Wycliffe's idea of creating an English Bible such a radical idea?

2. Briefly describe and explain the papal schism that occurred during Wycliffe's day.

3. Describe and explain the character and quality of Wycliffe's translation.

Long

1. What influence did Wycliffe's translation have on later English Bibles?

Quiz

1. (T/F) The name Wycliffe is today synonymous with the desire to read the Bible in its original language.

2. (T/F) Wycliffe's approach to the Bible was initially accepted by the Catholic Church.

3. (T/F) The idea of producing an English Bible was an attempt to overthrow tyranny.

4. (T/F) By the year 1075, the pope ruled over both church and state.

5. (T/F) A central theme in Wycliffe's theology is that all institutions are inherently flawed.

6. (T/F) While others wanted to undercut the foundation of the Catholic Church, Wycliffe sought to reform it internally.

7. (T/F) The Lollards' complaint against the Vulgate was that only the clergy could understand its language.

8. (T/F) Wycliffe translated the Bible into English from Greek texts.

9. (T/F) Possession of Wycliffe's English Bible was never allowed because it undermined Catholic authority.

10. (T/F) The instigators of the Peasants Revolt based their actions upon Wycliffe's teachings.

CHAPTER 9

The Bible and the Reformation

You Should Know

- Above all, humanism was an approach to learning.

- The humanists were not content to use the Vulgate because it was inadequate for true biblical studies, there were flaws in Jerome's translation style, the Vulgate was only a translation, and the Vulgate was not accurate at times to the Greek or Hebrew text.

- The study of Hebrew was frowned upon because those who spoke Hebrew eventually converted to Judaism.

- Erasmus has always been known as the prince of the humanists.

- *Sola Scriptura*: the principle that the Bible alone is the authority in matters of faith

- *Ad Fontes*: going back to the sources

Essay Questions

Short

1. What are the differences between Protestants and Catholics in their understanding of biblical authority? What are some of the main differences between most Protestant and Catholic Bibles?

2. What did the Latin phrase *ad fontes* signify for the study of the Bible? Why did many authorities in Europe disagree with the desire to read Greek and Hebrew texts?

3. Describe Erasmus's view of the Latin Vulgate and his relationship with the Catholic Church. What was Erasmus' major contribution to Greek studies?

Long

1. Describe humanism as practiced at the end of the Middle Ages. Describe in detail the various attitudes the humanists exhibited towards the Latin Vulgate.

Quiz

1. (T/F) Protestants and Catholics both agree on the principle of *sola scriptura*.

2. (T/F) Protestants typically scorn the Vulgate because it is based upon Greek, not Hebrew.

3. (T/F) The most influential movement at the end of the Middle Ages was humanism.

4. (T/F) Weaknesses in Jerome's Vulgate led humanists to study Greek and Hebrew in order to better understand the Bible.

5. (T/F) Protestant Bible translations were the result of the humanist movement.

6. (T/F) The main contribution of Erasmus was that he was the first person to inspire others to study Greek.

7. (T/F) The Complutensian Polyglot was a multi-volume book containing parallel Bible texts in Latin, Greek, and Hebrew.

8. (T/F) Erasmus produced his Greek text paired with the Latin Vulgate.

9. (T/F) Luther's translation would go on to have a more profound impact on the German language than any other single text.

10. (T/F) The Catholic response to Reformation criticisms of the Vulgate was the Council of Trent.

CHAPTER 10

The Protestant Bible in English

You Should Know

- Henry VIII was awarded the title "Defender of the Faith."
- Tyndale needed official sanction to begin his Bible translation.
- Tyndale's first Bible edition retained services of a publisher in Cologne. Tyndale planned to smuggle the printed Bibles into England, and he fled from persecution before the Bible could be printed.
- Thomas More was the leading English humanist of the sixteenth century, conducted a publishing campaign against Tyndale, and was a convinced Catholic.
- Tyndale has had the most influence on the English language since Chaucer.
- As many as 90 percent of all modern English translations still reflect the wording used by Tyndale.

Essay Questions

Short

1. What view did Tyndale share with Wycliffe, who came before him? Why was it difficult for Tyndale to produce a Bible in English?

2. What was the central issue in England that enabled Coverdale and others to create an English Bible and not be persecuted for it?

3. How was Tyndale's Bible perpetuated in later English translations?

Long

1. Describe some of the characteristics that were common to the Reformers who sought to create a Bible translation. Which of these characteristics are present in Christian leaders today?

Quiz

1. (T/F) The story of England and the Reformation is the story of Henry VIII's children and their shift between Protestantism and Catholicism.

2. (T/F) Tyndale pursued the right to translate the Bible into English.

3. Why did Tyndale have to start his Bible translation a second time?
   a) Catholic officials learned of his plan to smuggle Bibles to England
   b) Tyndale could not find a publisher for his Bible
   c) The Bibles were destroyed when the ship sank on the way to England
   d) The Bibles were stolen by a merchant named Humphrey Monmouth

4. (T/F) The Worms edition of the Tyndale Bible did not have commentary notes.

5. (T/F) Thomas More wrote works attacking Tyndale's Bible.

6. (T/F) Tyndale's Old Testament was not completed because he was martyred.

7. (T/F) The King James Bible borrowed nearly all of Tyndale's New Testament.

8. Tyndale created which of the following words that appear in our English Bibles?
   a) Atonement
   b) Yom Kippur
   c) Scapegoat
   d) Filthy lucre

9. (T/F) The first person tasked with creating a Bible for the English church was Thomas Cranmer.

10. (T/F) The Great Bible was based upon the Tyndale text and was authorized by Henry VIII.

CHAPTER 11

The King James Bible

You Should Know

- Conservative estimates are that as many as 50 percent of those who read the Bible on a weekly basis use the King James Bible.

- The original title page of the KJV read *The Holy Bible*.

- England during the time of Queen Elizabeth I had no pope, had two sacraments, condemned the Catholic teaching on purgatory, and stressed that the Bible should be published without the Apocrypha.

- Those who opposed the Anglican form of worship were often from Reformed churches.

- Puritans and Anglicans disagree over the following practices: robes, wedding rings, bowing before the cross, and making the sign of the cross.

- Before James I approved the idea of a new Bible translation, the Anglicans and Puritans disagreed over which theological notes were superior.

Essay Questions

Short

1. Describe some of the ways in which Anglicanism differed from Catholicism.

2. What was James I's primary problem with the Puritans? What was the Puritan response to James when he traveled to London to be crowned king?

3. What were the guidelines James laid down for a new, approved Bible translation? What is one contrast between the King James Bible translation style and that of the earlier Tyndale Bible?

Long

1. Why did the Reformed churches have such strong disagreement with the Anglican church? What were some of the main points, and do these same points continue as items of contention in the modern church?

Quiz

1. (T/F) In Britain the King James Version is called the Authorized Version.

2. (T/F) England was a Protestant nation by the time of Elizabeth I.

3. (T/F) The main point of contention between the Anglican and Reformed churches was worship.

4. (T/F) The Geneva Bible was designed as a successor to the Great Bible, but became a symbol of nonconformity under Elizabeth I.

5. (T/F) The Bishops' Bible was written as a smooth-flowing translation to compete with the wooden translation of the Geneva Bible.

6. (T/F) James I was raised as a Protestant, even though his mother was a Catholic.

7. (T/F) King James I agreed to approve a new translation, provided it contained notes and was based upon the Bishops' Bible.

8. (T/F) The King James Bible is not a fresh translation, but a revision of previous translations.

9. (T/F) The King James Bible is less formal than the English language spoken at the time.

10. (T/F) The use of different committees working on the King James Version resulted in the same words being translated in different ways or spelled differently.

CHAPTER 12

The Modern Bible Movements

You Should Know

- If the KJV was a masterpiece, it was a masterpiece with the flaws that come from the shortcomings of being human.

- The first serious attempt to populate the New World during Elizabeth's reign was the Roanoke Colony.

- The quality of Anthony Purver's Quaker Bible translation was lifeless.

- During the Reformation period, printers might assume their works would be copied by others, reprinted by other printers, and sold by other printers.

- Julia E. Smith Parker produced the first Bible entirely translated by a woman.

- One can no longer assume that men and women today have ever opened a Bible.

Essay Questions

Short

1. Is Jonathan Swift's praise for the KJV accurate? Why or why not?

2. What was the hope in England now that Protestants were established in the New World? What debates began in the New World as a result of the different denominations that were present?

3. Why did new Bible translations spring up in the New World?

Long

1. Explain the differences in thinking between translating a Bible version based upon the desires of a denomination and the needs of missionaries going to unreached people groups. Answer this question in light of the religious turmoil in Europe and the expansion of Christian denominations in America.

Quiz

1. (T/F) Settlers to the New World brought only English Bibles with them.

2. (T/F) America became a melting pot of denominations, many with their own Bibles.

3. (T/F) Many Puritans in the New World were accustomed to the Geneva Bible.

4. (T/F) Choosing a single Bible for a church or denomination creates a strong bond.

5. (T/F) The Family Bible was a successful marketing strategy, being both Scripture and a family heirloom.

6. (T/F) A uniquely European characteristic is for each denomination to have its own Bible translation.

7. (T/F) The method of Julia E. Smith Parker's translation was to be thoroughly consistent in translation so that verb tenses, for instance, always worked the same way.

8. (T/F) *Young's Literal Translation* came as a reaction to imperfections in the translation practices used in other Bible versions.

9. (T/F) Until the nineteenth century, the need for Bibles was for discipleship and training new Christians.

10. (T/F) Using the Bible as a tool for evangelism led to the necessity for the Bible translation to be more literal.

CHAPTER 13

The Bible Today–
And Tomorrow

You Should Know

- Numerous Bible societies have toiled to provide Bibles for the modern world.

- William Wilberforce was one of the leading voices for the founding of the British and Foreign Bible Society.

- The British and Foreign Bible Society distributed more than 150 million copies of the Bible annually in the latter half of the twentieth century.

- The British and Foreign Bible Society decided to remove the Apocrypha from its translations.

- The discoveries of older Greek manuscripts had materially changed only a handful of texts.

- The five English Bible families: Bibles in the King James family, Bibles in the RV family, Bibles in the NIV family, Bibles that stand alone, and New Vernacular Catholic Bibles

Essay Questions

Short

1. Why did many evangelicals fear the new revised Bible versions? Why did some lay Christians want to hold on to their KJV Bibles instead of using the new Bibles?

2. Why is it hard to imagine that any modern translation could avoid the critique of injecting bias into the translation?

3. What does it mean that a translation is gender-inclusive or gender-neutral? Do you think this is a positive or negative quality?

Long

1. What was the influence of the Bible societies on the printing and distribution of Bibles, compared to earlier translation and printing practices? Do you think translations today are more influenced or less influenced by denominational distinctions than they were centuries ago?

Quiz

1. (T/F) Modern Bible societies have driven up the cost of printed Bibles.

2. (T/F) The inspiration for the founding of the British and Foreign Bible Society was the lack of Bibles in the Welsh language.

3. (T/F) The British and Foreign Bible Society played an important role in modern Bibles when it made the decision to remove the Apocrypha from the translations.

4. (T/F) The American Bible Society was formed in 1816 to supply Bibles to the poor.

5. (T/F) One criticism leveled against the Revised Version was that it originated in England, not America.

6. (T/F) A crucial development behind the Revised Version was the publication of the Westcott and Hort Greek New Testament.

7. (T/F) The need for the Revised Standard Version was clear because of the backlash against the earlier RV and ASV versions.

8. (T/F) The NASB likely received less criticism because it claims to be the most literal translation in history.

9. (T/F) The most popular translation that uses a dynamic-equivalent approach is the New English Bible.

10. (T/F) Gender-inclusive translations have been criticized for making the Bible conform to today's modern culture.

Notes